W0254400

The Monster Trilogy

RM Vaughan

The Monster Trilogy

Plays by RM Vaughan

The Susan Smith Tapes

A Visitation by Saint Teresa of Avila upon Constable Margaret Chance

Dead Teenagers

Coach House Books

copyright © RM Vaughan, 2003

first edition

Published with the assistance of the Canada Council for the Arts and the Ontario Arts Council

NATIONAL LIBRARY OF CANADA
CATALOGUING IN PUBLICATION

Vaughan, R. M. (Richard Murray), 1965-
The monster trilogy / R.M. Vaughan.

ISBN 1-55245-132-1

I. Title.

PS8593.A94M66 2003 C812'.54 C2003-905250-8

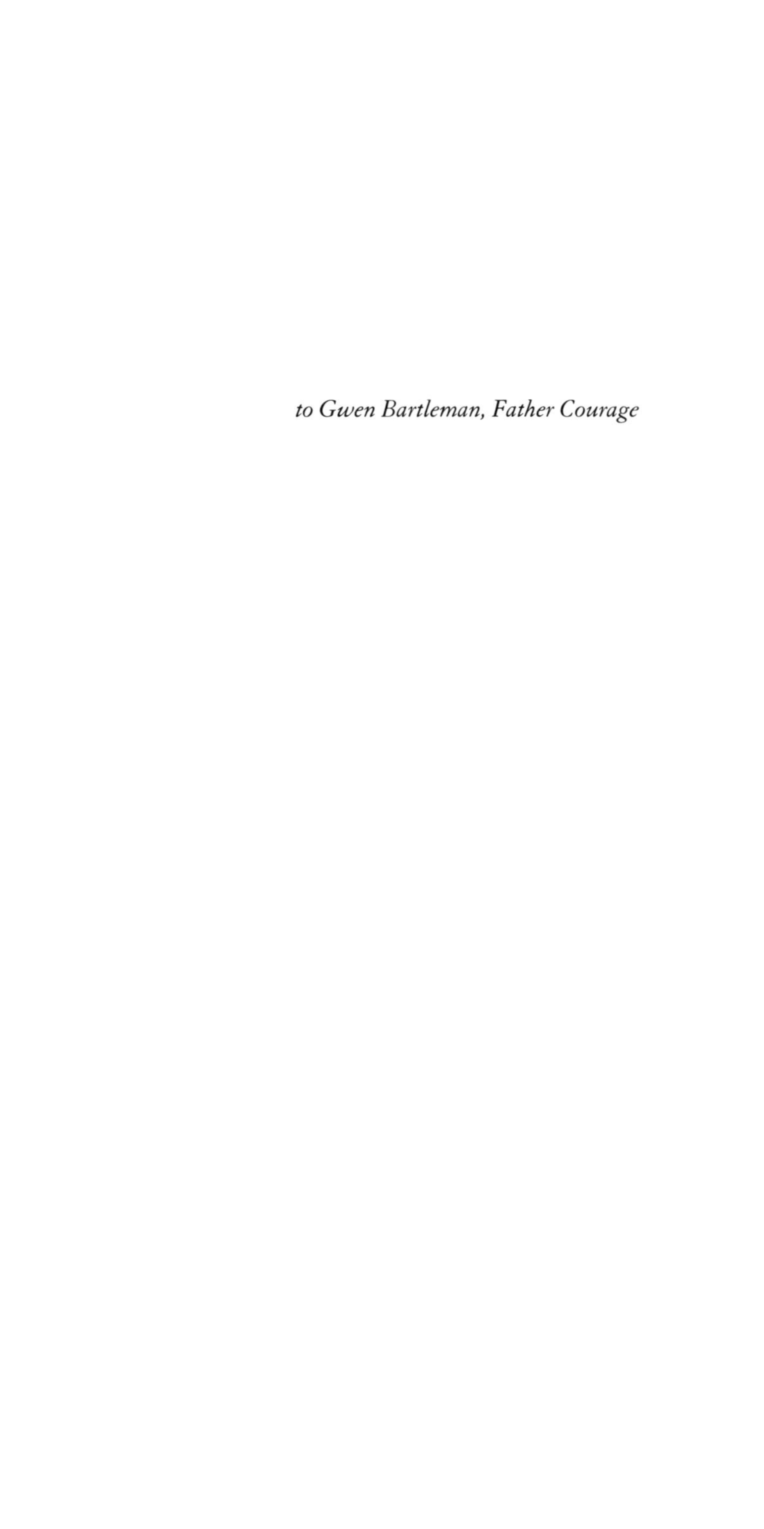

to Gwen Bartleman, Father Courage

Introduction

by Sonja Mills

Dear Richard,

Thank you so much for asking me to write the introduction to your brilliant *Monster Trilogy*. First of all, I love you, have I ever mentioned it? Don't think I've ever met a nicer guy, though you are cranky, suspicious, bitter and a bit of a gossip queen. But of course it is this very rare synthesis of personal traits, along with your love/hate relationship with theatre, and life itself, that makes us even remotely simpatico.

You have seen too much, my friend. Clearly. Too much theatre, too much film, too much art. How many times have I heard you say, 'I'm never writing another play'? Or, 'I'm never doing another art show'? You're full of shit, of course; you will continue to do all that and more, because you are a sucker for punishment and a truly gifted and dedicated artist and if people like you didn't do the stuff you're compelled to do we'd drown in a sea of *Lion King* (which did have fabulous costumes). I understand your instinct to run screaming from it all. Real art is hard and thankless. You're good at it, though. Good at all the machination and manipulation. I'm sure I could dig up a few cases in point from my personal files.

Did I read something at some stupid poetry gig in Northern Ontario once upon a time, or is it all just a horrible,

horrible daydream? Some skank bar called the Ferret and Gherkin, wasn't it? My god, more poets than poetry enthusiasts among the drunks at the Weasel and Pumpkin in James Bay. Bastard. You got me the gig so I'd drive you there, didn't you? I'm old and the details escape me anyway, so you may as well confess.

And do you remember when we were in Montreal and we both bought a bunch of old comic books? You turned yours into an art show with wine and cheese and photographers and the whole deal. Comic books! (And didn't you get a fat grant to do that show? Nice one.) I tried to sell mine for a dollar at a yard sale, but I only got a quarter cuz they were in French. See? You're good. And never the one dancing on the bar in your brassiere, either. How many times have you, Richard Vaughan, Ricardo Vaughantalban, who has more reason than any of us to be a raging alcoholic, been the only sober mortal in a roomful of gushing gargoyles at one of those ghastly theatre parties or insipid art openings? What is wrong with you?

Anyway, I just read your *Monster Trilogy* again. It makes me laugh till I pee and gives me the shitting creeps at the same time. Thanks for that, Richard, so glad to know you. Those wacky psychotic characters, with their cracked ideas about right and wrong – it is so sad and funny it makes me want to fall in love and kill my lover and then myself. In a good way. Thank you for being funny, not just telling jokes. Don't get me started, I've got a rage coming on. Though a knee to the groin will get a laugh every time, you my friend, you got the funny. Mmm, good carrot, lots of irony. Do you remember the opening of *The Susan Smith Tapes* at that whatever Rhubarb! festival it was? It was such a small venue, and I laughed

SOOO loud every time she referred to the brutal murder of her own children as 'the bad time' or 'the incident' that I actually made a bit of a spectacle of myself. Sorry about that. And *Margaret Chance*? Stop me now. That someone so racist and horrible could actually evoke an empathetic response when she complains that her husband won't go down on her is a sheer stroke of playwrighterly genius, Richard. High hilarity. And I pretty much laughed right over all that sick, perverted reverend's lines at *Dead Teenagers,* too. Oh well. You've ruined a few of my openings too, don't forget, but I don't hold grudges. (The little Sonja in my head is laughing, laughing, laughing at that last one.)

Ah, but Richard, I wank poetic, doesn't I? Never mind all that. What happened to us? You and me? I thought we had something going there in Montreal but you always came home at ungodly hours, smelling like strange men. I hate it when that happens.

Good luck with the art thing. In case of emergency there's always that knee-to-the-groin joke-writing gig; I understand TV will pay the rent if you'll lie down for it.

Your friend,
Sonja Mills

p.s. No, of course I won't write the introduction to your stupid book! I'm trying to make a shitty living writing stupid plays over here! *Phantom of the Opera* and a deli tray, that's what they want! Don't get me started.

The Susan Smith Tapes

Production History

This play was originally produced for the 1998 Rhubarb! Festival at Buddies in Bad Times Theatre, Toronto.

It was directed by Moynan King and starred Kirsten Johnson as Susan Smith.

The Susan Smith Tapes was made into a short film by Jeremy Podeswa in 2001 in a co-production by the Canadian Broadcasting Corporation, Rebel Films and Showcase Television.

Kirsten Johnson starred as Susan Smith.

Susan Smith sits on metal-framed bed in a bare prison cell. Her hair is pulled back into a ponytail. She wears a blue denim shirt and blue denim pants. The breast pocket of her shirt is numbered. Over her head is a single, dull light.

Smith sets up a video camera on a tripod in front of her bed.

SUSAN SMITH: Hello, Miss Oprah? I hope you can see me all right. I don't photograph too well. I mean, with these lights and all. And the white – white makes me look fat. Miss Oprah, I'm sending you this tape because I think maybe you never got near my last letter. It came back all bent up and ragged like a worn-out mop and I don't like to think you'd treat a heartfelt letter that way. I know you got some helpers on your show, so maybe it was one of them did it to my letter. Funny thing was, when I make the word 'heart' I don't spell it out h-e-a-r-t but I draw it directly on the paper, like a valentines heart *(draws heart with finger in the air)*, I always done that, since I don't remember when – and, well, when my last letter came back, somebody, well, somebody mean, took my letter and cut out every one of my signature hearts. Why do people do these things? Guess some folks can't forgive and forget. They say taking a piece of a person's handwriting is a way to do the voodoo on the person. Do you believe that?

Miss Oprah, I hope you still remember me. My name is Susan Smith, and I did a evil thing.

She stops the camera, rewinds for a few seconds, then starts again.

Miss Oprah, I know you still remember me. My name is Susan Smith. Evil things happened to me.

I have to talk to you in the video because I'm on sandwiches for the next two days. That's what we call it in prison when they suppose you might do harm to yourself. See, if you get on sandwiches, it means you don't get no fork or knife to eat with, seeing as you can take yourself down with even a plastic knife. And the warden says that goes for pens, too. There was a girl here who took a Bic out and worked the small end of the clear part on the bottom of her shoe till it was sharper than a snake's tongue and then she – well, never mind all that. So they give me the video instead, being my constitutional right to communicate through the United States Postal Service, but I was thinkin' there's sure lots more sharp parts on a video than an old fool Bic – but maybe there's people here who want to see me come to hurt, and then they can say nobody said nothin' about a video, and wasn't that Susan Smith smarter than we all thought, doing herself in with two little red buttons and a busted lens. You see, I ain't saying I never thought of my options.

Miss Oprah, I'm scared. So what, everybody's scared. I learned that here. But I'm scared of history. What are people gonna say about me in the future times? Miss Oprah, a lot of untrue stories have been said about me and

I need to have my time to make my say. I was a good mother to Michael and Alex, right up till the bad time. Those boys was always clean and dressed sharp and they never went hungry one minute of their lives. That is my truth. Can't nobody take that achievement away from me.

A loud splashing sound is heard by the audience, the sound of a car hitting a lake. Smith does not hear it.

Do you know that song 'Two Hearts Beat Like One'? Used to be my little joke that I was gonna rewrite it and make it 'Three Hearts,' for me and my babies, and make a million dollars. Fix everything. But we was like that, Three Hearts. Some days when they was at the playschool I'd just burst out cryin' and didn't know why and then they come home and the sitter, she'd say, 'Alex had hisself a stumble on the front steps, banged up his knee,' and I knew that's why I carried on crying before. I was connected. I felt those

boys inside me sure as they was still unborn in me. All day and all night. Every day. I was alive with them boys, Miss Oprah, and I nearly died with them too.

Sometimes I get hungry, right after supper, right on a full stomach, unsensible hungry, and then I says a little prayer to my angels up on God's lap. Momma hears you, boys, Momma hears your tummies rumblin'. Now you ask God for your supper. Beans and wieners. White bread with brown sugar. And then I ain't hungry no more.

I love my family, Miss Oprah. I trust you. Momma still talks about the day you came down from Chicago to visit the lake where my boys went to Glory. We don't see too much Hollywood in South Carolina. Momma said you was real ordinary like and still had your good Southern manners. I wish you hadn't brought your cameramen to the lake, though, because it's such a pretty lake and now the whole world only sees the bad side of the location. Maybe you and me can work together to make that old lake shine again.

I am good on TV. I come across natural.

The lights go out. Lights up on Smith sitting before the camera.

Mr. Springer, my name is Susan Smith. You did a show on me a few years back, and I'm just saying thank you again and a hello to you. I guess you can tell I'm still in prison. I gained some weight since you saw me last, from the sittin' all day. I was upset first about the extra pounds, but where am I supposed to be goin' for the rest of my life that I need to be pretty? Kinda a relief, just to let go. If I'm healthy, I thank the Good Lord for my fortune.

Mr. Springer, when the incident I done involving my two boys came out, there was a whole team of folks at the county District Attorney office workin' day and night to fix me for the electric chair but they lost. Listen to me! Of course they lost, 'cause here I am alive and jawin' away like a TV talk show person myself!

People down here say you are just another up-North liberal Jew, but I don't take account of that kind of talk. The world needs all creeds and colours. I saw you done a whole program on the badness of the death penalty, and I was thinking you should do another one because the issue is very large in the minds of many people. I can help out, if you like.

When my boys was killed, I took responsibility. I was slow to it, I admit, but eventually I come around to the truth. People say the best ways I can pay back for my boys is for me to go on over to the other side myself, but there's more than one way to make amends.

I want to come on your show and tell young mothers my story, so's they can learn from my example. That's what I feel all the men on the death row should be made to do, is to talk in public. Like a lecture. Say what they done and why they done it and be a lesson to others. If the State of South Carolina up and hauled me to the electric chair, they only get a one-shot deal on the example of my life. That's a sinful waste of the human spirit.

I been practicin' my set piece, and now I would ask you to hear it out.

She reads from a sheet of paper.

My name is Susan Smith, and I have experienced great tragedy in my life. The death of a child is every mother's worst all-time day and nighttime nightmare. The death of two children is double that plus some traumas nobody can name. I am here today to tell all you kind people that human life is precious and unreplaceable. I know because I will never hear my baby boys' voices again. I will never see them goin' off for the first day of school, never help

them with learnin' their times tables, never go down to the front porch to meet their girlfriends and never hold their own babies in my arms. Life is cruel and beautiful too, but the cruellest day in the world came when circumstances situated to take my babies from me. Even after I am dead and gone I can still hold my head up high to the sky above and say no matter what, I am a mother, and that is a no-refund deal.

She sets the paper down.

Well, it's just a start. I was always better at writin' Christmas cards than whole letters. A message of love is the shortest breath, my momma used to say. What do you think? I'm bashful to admit that I copied the sound of it from them mini-stories you tell at the end of your show. Hope you don't take no offence.

The sound of two baby boys screaming is heard. Smith does not hear it.

Mr. Springer, I don't deserve to die. There is women in here who killed their husbands who was beatin' on them, and women who killed for money, and women who killed by accidents, and ain't one of us needs to sit in a metal chair with our hair shaved off to understand we done wrong in God's eyes. My boys and me, we had a special bond. We was like people who can talk to each other without saying a word, them gifted people with angel powers. I couldn't walk away from that power, Mr. Springer, nobody in the world could. My mother love was too strong. Them boys woulda spent the rest of their lives wondering why they was so bad that their momma put herself at the bottom of the lake rather than be with them. I would have put a curse on my own children had I gone to Glory before my time. I admit to my shame I wanted to commit suicide, but I did not leave my boys abandoned, I did not take the easy road and leave my babies to make on in the world without a mother.

I made a choice, for my babies. That's what folks is afraid of, the deep-down feelin' they got that they don't wanna hear talkin' to them – the voice that says Susan Smith done right, horrible right, but right. It's too hard to bear.

I made a choice, in a second, in a half a minute, and it moved the world to tears.

That's why they lost on the death penalty. 'Cause it's psychological. Wrong in the heart don't cousin with right in the brain. Anybody wants to come kill me better look

around and ask hisself when was the last time he sacrificed like I sacrificed for my babies. Most people won't even put a sick dog down, they's so selfish. I am not afraid to cry on Wednesday so I can smile on Sunday.

That's the problem with the electric chair – it don't look to the future. It don't calculate for the limitless quality of the human potential. All my life, I have always looked to the horizon, not the trail.

Mr. Springer, I sometimes think I am the bravest woman I know. Please contact me care of the warden when you get a chance to watch this tape. Thank you and goodbye for now.

She shuts off the camera. The lights go down. Smith sits in front of the camera.

You may not remember me – I guess my story's old news to you folks up in New York – but my name is Susan Smith. I was watching your program *20/20* last night on the night guard's TV and it was a repeat of a show you did three years ago on my hometown, after my babies were found.

I liked the way you walked around the lake, like it was a sacred place, which it is to me, and the way you talked, sorta soft and sorta hard at the same time, like a mother. If I may suggest something, Miss Walters, I think your decision to wear jewellery down at the lake was right and proper. I understand that with your people there is a custom of wearing personal ornamentation as a sign of respect for the dead. I'm only bringing this up 'cause some folks in town said they thought you was crass, but that town is full of ignorant people who never been nowhere in the world.

Miss Walters, I liked the way you described the candles folks left by the lake – you said they was like 'tiny sparks of life for two tiny lives that were snuffed out early,' and that is so true. My babies went to God like birthday candles, special and bright and just the right size, but only on for a minute before the wish comes and puts out the flame. I think if you ever came here to see me you and me would get along real good – we both got sensitivities.

Because you spoke to my heart last night, I want to come on my own private TV show here *(laughs)* and try to speak to yours. I don't have the way with poetry like you got, but my heart is a open page. The prison don't have a proper visiting room like you'd be accustomed to, and I'd be embarrassed to let you talk to me in the exercise yard 'cause it ain't nothing but a flat patch of concrete with a basketball hoop, so if you want to just show this video on the *20/20* show, I won't mind.

I never wanted this kind of national attention, but I got it anyway, so I may's well get in my say in the story.

Miss Walters, I believe life is about decisions. Have you ever made a decision that took only a couple of minutes but changed the rest of your days? I did. That's the power of decisions, there's no goin' back, no bridge back across. Time gets pressed together, and whatever you do seems like just a baby step, but it's really a jump to the moon.

When I left my home on Tuesday, October 25, 1994, I was very emotionally distraught. I was a girl in a woman's body. I couldn't sort out my needs. I understand that now. I am learning to separate my temporal needs and my long-term goals. I wish I had that kind of sense in me that night.

My boys – Michael, he's three, and Alex, the baby, he's fourteen months – got in the back of the car like always. Michael says, 'Lock the doors, Momma!' – he always said that. It was our automobile safety game. I showed him how to fix his baby brother into the car seat so that he was safe and snug as a Eskimo papoose. Michael had a little First Reader book about the Eskimos he liked to look at. When we get in the car I say, 'Where's my Eskimo baby?' and Michael says, 'Here, Momma, all tied up.' Smart as can be. I'm like Michael, I do things by habit.

We drove around for four hours, the boys were asleep. There was something in the smell of the rain, something like gasoline but not as strong, something like dead leaves, like winter coming, and it made me sad.

I wanted to see the lake, the lake is so alive. If you go at night, you can watch the catfish jump for bugs and it makes you feel energetic. The lake's full of catfish. But lately folks don't eat them like they used to, they say the lake's poisoned forever. People are full of hate.

I sat by the side of the lake while the boys slept and snored and talked baby dream talk to each other and I thought to myself, I want to die. It just came over me, the death pull. I'm like that, just get taken away by emotions.

My problem is I don't know when to stop the stories. You know, like when you go to the bank and you're short five or ten dollars and instead of just shrugging it off you tell yourself that this one moment is a tiny picture of your whole life, like the next thing will be a parking ticket, and then you'll be late to get home, and then you'll get a bad bill in the mail or maybe lose your job or pick up the phone and hear that your best friend is dead – and the whole slide down started right there, at that silly bank counter and you are powerless, powerless like a Eskimo baby all tied up. I used to make up those stories every day, it's called Narrative Cognition Disorder. I wish I knew about it at the lake.

There is a very quiet repeat of the sound of a car crashing into lake, as well as the sounds of boys crying. Smith does not hear the sounds.

I felt I couldn't be a good mom any more. But I didn't want my children to grow up without a mom. I had to end our lives to protect us from any grief or harm.

The car went in no trouble. The mud around the lake is so slick. I only had to push it three or four times. Michael woke up for a minute.

'Where we goin', Momma?'

He never said another word, smart as can be. 'I love y'all! I love y'all! I love y'all!' He knew.

The sounds of the crash and the boys repeat, louder. Smith does not hear them.

I sat down on the beach, by the picnic tables, empty as air. I kept thinking somebody would come along and stop the accident, somebody would save me and my babies, somebody who really cared about me. But I was alone, what else is new.

Then the car flipped over, turned on its left side and went upside down. Only took a minute. I could see the tops of Michael and Alex's heads, their hair standing straight up, like on the Zipper ride at the state fair, and I thought they must be having fun, they must be giggling. And I thought, I'll just hop right in and we'll go down together. Upside down monkey bars.

The sounds of the crash and the boys repeat, very loud. Smith does not hear them.

If you was gonna drown, wouldn't you want to go without a struggle, wouldn't it be better to have no ability to fight, wouldn't it be peaceful?

I went to the lake and I put my hand on the surface of the water. All I could think about was a catfish coming up and taking one of my fingers for a worm. I flicked one finger, then all of them. No bites. It wasn't my time to go. The car was completely upside down. I realized I never saw the underside of a car before. You see, it wasn't my time to go.

The sounds of the crash and the boys bear down on the audience; the remainder of the text is shown on a monitor, from Smith's video.

Later on, after I came here, a policeman told me that the car going over like that was a blessing 'cause the boys took in the water upside down. Faster than right side up, he said. Painless, he said. Not painless for me, I felt like sayin', but he was tryin' to be nice and all. When there's a tragedy, folks say stupid things thinkin' it's comfort.

But you know that already, Miss Walters, you hear it every day.

END

A Visitation by Saint Teresa of Avila upon Constable Margaret Chance

Production History

A Visitation by Saint Teresa of Avila upon Constable Margaret Chance was originally produced for the 1996 Rhubarb! Festival at Buddies in Bad Times Theatre, Toronto.

It was directed by Franco Boni. It starred Ann Holloway as Constable Chance and Peter Lynch as Saint Teresa of Avila.

A golden crown is momentarily visible to the audience. It disappears.

Constable Chance sits at a doughnut-shop table. She is in full police uniform.

CONSTABLE CHANCE: No ... no! No more. I'm being swallowed alive here!

Pause.

I know the story. I know every shitting detail. It's burned in the back part of my brain, the animal part. He fucked her first – correction, he raped her first, then the other stuff. I know 'cause I'm related. To the perpetrator.

His cousin is my half-stepsister and the half-stepsister's uncle had two brothers, one of them being my uncle. So he's my half-stepcousin something – I don't exactly know ...

I recognized him. Met him at a wedding, years ago. He was quiet, almost stupid. He took the girl over to the Beaches and he raped her, rough raped her, and yes, he cut her head off. That part's true. Hacksaw. Cuts her head off and tosses it in the kiddies' sandbox for the dogs to eat. Drives over to the Mac's for a bag of chips after. Quiet as a mouse – quiet, fast, clean ... ugly as the mouth of hell. And I'm related. Distant, but related.

The boys got him two days later. Holed up in the basement, talking about God. It gives me the creeping shits. I mean, what if it's a gene, right, like a genetic predispatation to kill and it runs in the family? I could pass it on to my boy, Bradley.

Maybe I got a thread of this gene – that's all it takes, one bad link in the chain – say I'm in the middle of the hot and hornies and the gene kicks in, right, the Kill Gene, kicks right the fuck into my head and I gotta do a violence? I gotta cut off a pair of nuts or an arm or a whole head? Whaddya gonna do, you can't deny your genetic destiny.

So, here is the final unholy question: am I guilty?

A golden arrow is momentarily visible. It disappears. Constable Chance does not see it.

I got a prediction tits are gonna get bigger in the next generation. 'Cause of the global warming.

The world's getting hotter and hotter, so, there's like no rain for months and months – nothing grows. So people start living off breast milk again, like they did in Biblical times.

It makes perfect sense.

In twenty years tits will be like commodities, traded on the stinking stock exchange. Like gold.

I got thirty million Swedish hooters at five bucks a tit, I'll sell ya twenty million Norwegians at three bucks a tit. And the Japanese, eh, this will be their economic downfall.

They'll be coming to us for trade again, just like before, and we'll be like, 'Take the fucking Walkman back and hole it, Mr. Yamamoto, we're feeding the world.' Mark my words. I will be a very foolishly rich woman if I live long enough.

It's like the whole human race is turning in on itself. Hormone shots, dykes having babies, cock extensions – you ever notice there's no vagina extension? I mean, what if you got the peanut twat?

My friend Adele, I love her dearly but she's got no vulva as far as I can see. We went swimming once and I did the underduck on her and I thought, Holy Mary, if the water's magnifying my vision she's got problems. Like a keyhole with a lid.

I don't agree with all this rearranging of God's gifts. The body is a cathedral. You don't walk in and rearrange the Stations of the Cross 'cause the ending's better.

The human body is sacred. That's why I wear this badge. Sacred.

A dove is momentarily visible. It disappears. Constable Chance does not see it.

My son, Bradley, is forbidden to walk the street in them spandex biker pants, the Ball Bras I call them. I seen this guy from 52 Division with them on at the Brotherhood of

Armed Officers and Guardians barbecue – Rashad Meshad Shranalanga Dong Ding or some fucking nine-inch name with a comma in the middle. What the hell kinda name has a comma in the middle – a name's not a sentence, it don't need punctuation.

My Bradley ever walk in the door with the Ball Bra on he's flat, flat out, flat on his ass. Like Rashad there, you can see everything an' they're fucking big. But those people got to have big balls 'cause of the hot weather at the equator. The humidity down there makes it hard to have babies so evolution has naturally given these people bigger reproductive equipment.

Figure it out – it's 100 goddamn degrees every day and you gotta lug papayas on yer head every damn morning to feed the family and do you want to be dragging some kid around inside you for nine months?

I was pregnant in the summer, take my word – sweat, puke, shits all day, sweat some more.

So when the man comes along to plant the seed the woman's body is naturally resistant. But he's got the boulder balls going and you're mesmerized – 'cause there's no stopping what's inside the double barrels and now you gotta drag some kid plus the goddamn papayas too. But these women got longer arms. Nature takes care of them too.

It's God's master plan for the world. It's fair – it's hard, but it's fair.

My darling Bradley boy, he thinks he's too big for a little correction. I told his Your Eminence, I told him, 'Give it to the little shit right across the ass.' Ahh, the husband's a loser.

I'd do the necessary evils myself but I don't wanna warp his sexuality.

My Bradley could go fruit on me if he don't get a sensible amount of male authority inflicted on him. He goes fruit, or he turns out one of those losers needs some bitch to kick his ass for him to get off. All my fault.

It's a lot of heart-bleeding responsibility. What if he catches me and the husband doing it? The husband says, 'Let him watch, it's natural' – like I actually want a natural child. No thank you. Go up to the Annex sometime and catch the Natural Child parade passing by.

What I would like to understand is what's with the gypsy clown outfits – patches, patches, patches. I got no problem with a little vibrancy, but keep it to two colours, three max.

And everything's gotta come from some women's co-operative labour camp in Argentina and have a hole in it. It's like you know these kids are sitting in the parents' basement calculating where to put the next really fucking spiritual hole in their pants – 'On my crotch, on my ass, on my elbow, where oh where shall my hole of righteous poverty go?'

And I hate the little weed bags from Africa swinging around their necks. White kids as pale as the fresh blowing December snow and they're wearing a weed bag from Mother Africa.

I hauled one in last month and she says, no joke, 'It's part of my religion.' I'll kick some religion into her right quick.

God help me I end up with some commie, vegetarian, bisexual son who hangs around the Kensington Market all day selling the freaking *Internationalist Worker's Labour Front* newsletter – and why? – all because my loser husband thinks the kid should learn the birds and bees from his loving parents.

I sacrifice my pleasure 'cause if there's kids in the house you gotta calm yourself or they see too much too fast. My Bradley is gonna be deviationally unwarped by the time he's eighteen no matter if he's got mutilator sex criminal genes in the family tree.

It could be one of those recess genes, the kind that skip a generation. Like twins.

There's twins every third generation because the twin gene is like, split or defracted or some shit so there can't be any twins having twins. 'Cause they'd come out retarded, these twin twins, 'cause they'd be, like, one-fourth of a full human being.

Let's say you are a twin. You and your brother. You have two boys, also twins. And your brother has two boys, more twins again. Now there's like six of you, all look exactly the same, and that's way too much commonality in the gene pool. It ain't healthy. It's like incest – the kids come out pale and flat-looking, like they got no blood.

I busted this creep once was doing his two daughters – both, if you please, knocked right up like two stuffed pigs – and the dutiful daughters bring the babies to the trial six months later while I'm giving my unholy testimony. So I look over and there's these two fucking baby aliens – both of them got eyes the same colour as this table and there's a weird light all around them. I mean, they were actually kinda sweet. Two retard day-glo babies and the survivor sisters, huddled together like it was some horrible accident their old man got caught on top of them under the *Lion King* bedspreads.

Those girls looked like refugees. It's genetics, eh? Don't screw with the genetics.

A golden chalice is momentarily visible. It disappears. Constable Chance does not see it.

I wonder if Rashad the Meshad the Mighty Balls believes he was a rat in a previous life, or a butterfly, or a Louis the Fourteenth reclining armchair? I got nothing against weird religions, just don't bring it into the squad room with you. Keep it at home.

Next thing we gotta put plastic Buddhas in every goddamn paddy wagon so's when we arrest our good friends in the Asian community they'll feel welcome and integrated into the police services. I'm sorry, but do you see the Virgin Mary hanging over my locker? No, you do not. Keep it at home, I say, keep it at home.

The husband's a fucking infidel. Won't go to church, won't pray. 'I ain't gettin' on my knees to no faggot priest,' he says. I'd like to see my godless husband on his sweet knees on my beautiful bedroom floor, then I'd be a happy woman. A woman deserves a little adventure.

It never ceases to amaze me men will do anything with their tongues except a muff. Open a beer bottle, sure, right to the teeth. It's only been fingered by thirty or forty nose-picking factory workers. Suck the gas out of a tank, sure, give him the hose. Gas will only chew the freaking lining out of his intestinal track.

But give his very clean and worship-deserving wife a little tongue dial around the flaps and Jesus – you'd think I was running bare twat over the counter at the methodone clinic.

I wonder if Rashad the magnificent goes down on the wife?

These Hindus, they got 60,000 sexual positions figured out – 30,000 of them exclusively for the tongue. It's in their book, *Arabian Nightlife*.

Pages and pages of people going at it – the double swan, the broken camel backflip, the lion with three mouths, the stretched starfish fist fuck – you name it, they got a way to do it.

Figured it out thousands of years ago, at the pinnacle of their culture. 'Cause the royal families had, like, maybe thirteen people in the whole kingdom was good enough for them to copulate, so they had to think up 60,000 ways to make it or the royal family would get bored and die out and then the whole culture would disappear.

In ancient times it was against the law to do it and not give pleasure to the woman. Punishable by death and torture. 'Cause women are the nurturing life force of the cosmos. It all comes back to the mother.

Did you ever see that Jodie Foster movie where little snot bag Jodie kills her old man and turfs him in the basement and then she kills, like, half the dogshit town and throws them in the cellar too?

Why? All the way through the movie I'm going, why? Why the hell is she doing it? And then it comes to me. The husband's asleep on the couch and it comes to me. I'm thinking, lookit my lazy-ass husband dragging his gut over the sectional – and I go, what if my Bradley was suddenly a widow child and only had this lump of carcass to look after him?

And I says, shit, it's 'cause she's got no mother.

Jodie's got no mother so she has never learned by example to control her natural feminine anger.

It's all in the mother.

But you gotta rise above. Like Rashad – so what if he worships monkeys and three-headed elephants? He can put on a pair of decent pants, can't he?

People can control themselves.

Otherwise it's gonna be anarchy. Freaking chaos. Nobody's responsible for nothing, so nobody's gotta fix nothing.

What if some New Canadian's six-armed snake god tells him he's gotta beat on the wife? What if the wife thinks whatever the snake god says is OK by her? Whaddya gonna do, arrest the godless plastic snake infidelity, confiscate the stinking incense?

Didja ever go in one of these houses with the shitting godless incense burning and you wonder how the hell the house keeps from catching fire? Mercy, the sweet soapy reek of it all – like a room fulla housewives up at Yonge and Israel.

There's gonna be a whole generation of Asian kids with the wheezing asthma 'cause of the incense. And we gotta pay the medical bills. And then they can't work 'cause of the asthma. So we hand over the lovely welfare. And then they go sue the parents for negligent exposure to burning festive fucking perfumed substances. Of course, we gotta pay the court costs 'cause we have already established they got no money in the first place.

I say, OK, the ones that's here already, fine. I can handle that. My Bradley even brings a few over for the Nintendo. But no more, no more. The real Canadians are disappearing. I'm being swallowed alive here.

I got no problem with mixing for fun but it's the babies I worry about.

What are they, black, white? Nobody knows. All mixed the fuck up 'cause some tighty whitey got herself browned just to finish off what's left of her poor, harassed parents.

My Bradley – he's only nine but we had a talk about race relations and I says Bradley can do what he likes but I am not tossing brown rice at no Island girl and calling my blessed grandchildren Botswana or Kintakwah or Sister X.

No way's my Bradley gonna bring me home no problem grandchild I gotta arrest later for smoking happy rocks outside the Rasta Palace. If I got anything to say about it I will not have to bear that particular multicultural cross.

I will love my child and my child's child. It's his choices I don't have to love.

A golden scroll is momentarily visible. It disappears. Constable Chance does not see it.

My Bradley could have that recessor gene, the Killer Gene. I mean, anybody could have it. It's a distant relation, but …

Okay, like two weeks ago, I was mixing hamburgers to take to the beach and barbecue – I got the dried oregano and the dried onion and the dried basil and the dried garlic salt and the Campbell's tomato soup mix – all the good stuff – and I'm folding it in, getting my hands in the meat 'cause the meat was cool, cool on the hands, you know, from the fridge.

Not like ice cold but just cold, like tap-water cold. It felt good and soft in my fingers, 'cause my fingers they get right dry and hard from the car, from the steering wheel, from driving all the time and Jesus it's nice to get some relief.

I had all the time in the world and I guess maybe I closed my eyes for a minute and just felt ... cool.

I reach over for the salt and there's my Bradley behind me with his eyes fixed on my hands like something stunned him. Kids get right catatonical sometimes. It's the TV does it. So I'm looking at him and I'm smiling and saying, 'Hi honey, lookit the good hamburgers Mommy's making.' But, I'm not there – far as he's concerned, I am not present. My hands, though, he can't take his eyes off my hands.

I got real self-conscious about all the red, the red between my fingers, that dirty red you get from frozen meat. 'Cause from the freezing the blood is, like, brown and green.

Bradley sees me lookin' at my hands and he comes around, puts his little hands right into the hamburger, just like that, and I says, 'Is my Bradley gonna help Mommy make the hamburgers?' But he's holding my wrists, he's got his fingers tied up with mine like cat's cradle and it hurts, hurts 'cause he's holding my fingers hard, real hard, fingers turning white. He's, like, mesmerized.

So I says, 'Bradley don't hurt me.' I start thinking crazy shit like I'm stuck, I'm stuck ... it's a trap. Run. Run.

Foolish thoughts, like danger thoughts. Bradley will not look up at me, and I try to call the husband, try to wake the husband 'cause my brain's going, 'Call the hospital, Bradley's having a spasm, call the hospital.'

My baby, my baby, my baby … brain damage, annurisiams, gimp for life … I gotta wake the husband 'cause Bradley's got the death grip on me and I'm stuck to him and the hamburger is getting warm and smells like sweat and the spices are too strong, I'm gonna faint.

I was gonna faint, for the first time in my whole life. Pass out on my own kitchen floor and take my baby Bradley down with me …

Jesus … the whole world's on a bad corner … a blind, sharp corner … there's no brakes, no stopping … And he lets go, lets go … walks off and turns on the TV.

The husband finally wakes the fuck up, coulda been an hour later, I dunno, 'cause I'm lost. The meat's melted, turned to soup. The husband says, 'Why you breathing heavy – you having one of your multiples?'

I lost it, just crying and shit, and I don't do that.

'Cause it's in the family, eh?

And the husband, he thinks everything's Okay long as the kid's not on drugs, but there's worse shit than drugs.

Psychological shit, brain chemical stuff … problems in the blood …

St. Teresa of Avila appears in the sky. She is glowing. Constable Chance sees the miracle.

END

Dead Teenagers

Production History

Dead Teenagers was originally produced for the 2002 Rhubarb! Festival at Buddies in Bad Times Theatre, Toronto.

It was directed by Moynan King and it starred Caroline Gillis as the Reverend.

The Reverend paces before a row of chairs, fidgeting with an unlit cigarette. She is nervous and speaks to herself as if praying. She is fortyish and dressed in clerical attire.

REVEREND: Inches from sin, miles to Heaven. Inches from sin, miles to Heaven. Inches from sin, miles to Heaven. Inches from sin – 'Who am I?' How dare she ask me such a question.

Who am I, indeed!

Inches from sin, miles to Heaven.

That bitch, bitch! How dare she, how dare she! Bitch, hell bitch! Who am I, indeed!

The Reverend abruptly tucks the cigarette into her pocket.

Your Eminence, lovely to see you. Forgive my little vice, I know it's practically a capital crime to indulge in Sir Walter Raleigh's favourite habit. And with so many other things to worry about in the world today. But I digress.

The Reverend takes a seat.

I understand you have some questions regarding the little upset last weekend at young Bobby MacAbee's funeral. Let me assure you I am as keen to get to the bottom of this matter as you are. Most distressing. I don't know what got into me.

I'm bedevilled, that's what it is. I haven't been regular lately. I need to attend to myself with some sensible regimen of diet and sleep or my duties suffer. I'm aware of my failings, Your Eminence, very aware. I'm a cloudy winter window in good need of vinegar and brown paper.

The boy's mother certainly did put up a stink. I never imagined she'd call you. But here we are.

And I do feel for the bereaved, I always do. Perhaps in excess. What a terrible thing, to lose a child so young, a child with so much to see, so many mud pies to fool with, scraps and tussles and loves. Little loves and big, lifelong loves. But the child goes to Glory and who's left behind to cry and wail – the parents.

That poor MacAbee boy. The newspaper said the fencepost stuck clean through his heart. Like an arrow. I've never agreed with snowmobiles, especially with children. But then, at that speed I expect it was painless. You scream along the snow with nothing supporting you but a whisker of metal no bigger than a dog's leg. Who in Heaven knows what's under all that clean white snow? Rocks, fallen trees, hibernating bears. It's not safe. I heard he didn't even see the fence. Too much snow. There's whispers about beer and cigarettes, but that kind of talk doesn't help anyone now.

Poor boy. The post was frozen inside him when the Mounties found him, all the blood crystallized like a string of garnets on his chest. The men had to saw him out. The post went clean through his heart. I wonder if the snow anaesthetized his skin, I wonder if he heard the motor go cold, the birds in the trees. Maybe he thought the birds were angels singing him to God. There – I'll hold that picture in my head today. A handsome, strong boy frozen in rapture, songs to God's Mercy ringing through the pine trees. No pain at all, skin as white as Irish linen.

I sent Mrs. MacAbee a card with a sweet poem. But she was so busy with the funeral arrangements and all. I expect she'll respond in time.

Now, mind you, with my last two funerals I knew the families. Not well, of course, but I knew them. So they had to let me in. I mean, accept my support. They had to offer me a sandwich, had to hear my words of comfort. I performed a small prayer, not a full service, and I don't do the Latin unless people ask – nobody wants the Latin any more – but I did get to give a few of my best rhyming psalms, the easy ones. Families don't want an unwieldy tangle of poetry during the painful hours. A nursery rhyme is better than an epic.

Oh, but I'd love to do a real barnburner of a eulogy one day – all sorts of terror and blood and love tossed together. Scare the horse feathers off those old biddies from the Congregation Council, the Misery Mollies I call them – professional mourners.

Now, Your Eminence, do not look shocked – you know the type: old goats with nothing better to do than to show up for every crib death or leukemia baldy.

I swear they thrive on the gloom, and the free sandwiches. You can see them sucking the life juice out of the bereaved, sucking away like leeches on the skin of human sorrow.

You and I have a job to do, we have a function.

How dare they look at me that way, like I was diseased.

The Reverend sits down, waits for a response. An awkward silence opens up in front of her. She digs in her pockets.

Do you mind?

The Reverend fidgets with a new cigarette. She begins to light her cigarette then stops abruptly, puts it away.

Of course, of course! How thoughtless of me! Your asthma … Dreadful condition.

I love to watch smoke curl. I tried for years to smoke like Jayne Mansfield – through the nose. French inhalation, I believe it's called. She died young too … a car crash … cut off her head.

In the Shinto religion, smoke is used to give gifts to the departed. It's the cutest thing. The families burn tiny paper cars, paper hats, paper watches, paper money, paper kitchen sets and whole paper houses.

Quick as a monkey, up in smoke they go, off to Japanese Heaven. Imagine the clutter in a Shinto heaven. Every day must be like Christmas for deceased Japanese. I myself would find such constant reverence and adulation a bit of a wear and tear. I mean, I expect the afterlife to be peaceful, not a yard sale. However, I do believe things pass between the dead and the living. But I do not fully agree with the concept of the transference of materiality into the hereafter –

Oh! Of course, Your Eminence! We're not here to discuss ecumenical issues.

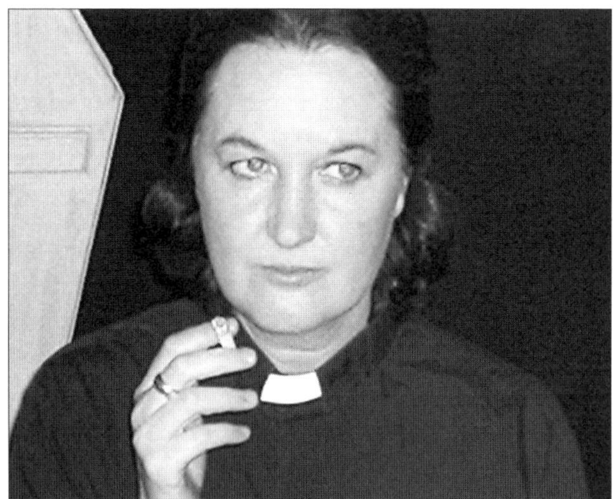

Pardon me, I will try to stay with the problem at hand. I realize your time is valuable, and I do understand how hard it is to please the church council.

Your Eminence, you know I do not enjoy complaining – but the church council has consistently voted down my approaches for a raise in my per annum. I'm supposed to live like a mouse, warming my hands over a rusty kettle and hoping for spring. God's work for donkey pay. I told the church council last year to either buy me a wood stove for the rectory or I would consider relocating.

Well, my stove finally did arrive. But what a lot of smoke it made at first, for such a small wood stove. Five false alarms. The fire department knows me by my face. One rather surly fireman suggested I could at least have coffee ready for them, as they have to make the trip anyway. But that's our classless society. Rude, lazy, smart-mouthed, overpaid brutes.

After the last little incident, the Fire Chief suggested to me that I was developing an unhealthy affection for the sound of midnight sirens. I am a woman of God, I said, I aspire to Heaven, not the Lake of Fire. That always shuts them up.

I wasn't bred to survive discomfort. The fire makes such a pleasing glow – pumpkin orange and pomegranate red, with some azure underneath and tiny clouds of blue smoke. A candy store come alive. Dancing hot sugar treats.

A fire is a comfort, a fire fills you up inside. And I need fortification because I'd swear to Our Lord Above that I'm shrinking, shrinking by ounces, thimblefuls and mosquito bites. Down, down to nothing.

I felt it last week, Your Eminence, the shrinking. A quick jerk in my bowels, a sudden increase in the density of me – thought I'd swallowed a needle.

The Reverend pauses, appears to lose touch with where she is.

I'm fading, Your Eminence, disappearing … like all the missing children. Every day there's new graves, shovels, grey mud and tears. Perfect, clear spring water tears. And golden hair, tied with black ribbon.

I love my work, Your Eminence. But can't you feel it, can't you feel the molecules moving between people, between things?

The whole world is covered in bits and pieces of the rest of the world. Can't you feel the flakes on your fingertips? I can. We're all passing molecules. It's like loving. Loving you can't avoid, can't hold back. A love that just happens and happens and there's nothing anyone can do.

That poor boy, his heart pierced clean through. Where did the sound of his heart go, his last pump-pump? Into the cold air with nobody to cherish the rhythm except the birds, the trees, the snow. Molecules.

The MacAbee funeral was flawless. Every lad in the school turned out in a good suit and the girls wore decent skirts. Hardly any garbage on the street. The hearse glided by like ice skates on a frozen pond. Followed by black cars, clean black cars. Such a lovely job on the boy's face, too. Sharp haircut, off the forehead, not too greasy. No hint of disrespect. The Lord Himself silenced the wind – you could hear tears dropping on the church steps. So much quiet, it was intoxicating.

I offered my comfort to his father. I was very respectful. I was exactly halfway down the church steps, not being a member of the family. I reached out. The air between us was cold, cold like a shock. I touched his shoulder and my chest shrunk inside me, an inward tug.

Molecules, Your Eminence. Strangers sharing molecules.

The boy was beautiful. Breaking into pieces, whirling specks ... free as pollen in August.

The Reverend pauses, collects herself.

Last summer there were so many deaths. God's mercy was not evident. Remember the two Wilson girls, crushed under a tractor? Playing the fool with heavy machinery. I wonder where the guidance is. Both killed instantly.

I offered my prayers to Mr. Wilson, but men like to be left alone. I've learned over the years – leave the men alone for six months, then they never shut up. But one can't find fault.

Of course Mr. Wilson wanted closed caskets. Two identical closed caskets, with awful, gawky high school photographs set on top. I hate closed caskets.

I understand the necessity, but surely something from the body is intact enough to look at? A hand, a cheek, a profile, or at least the eyes, peeking out.

Closed-casket services lack finality. You just don't know who's in there. We could be burying a load of gassed dogs from the Humane Society and you'd never know.

I meant to speak my mind about the issue – to me a closed casket is a door shut in your face. Like I say, I was prepared to clear the air with Mr. Wilson about the closed casket but I was so appalled by his behaviour that I could not function properly.

My Lord, Your Eminence, the wailing! Screeching like a farm animal in a burning barn. I'm certain he attempted to force himself to faint when the caskets were brought out of the chapel. Endless tears, waterfalls of tears, teeth-chattering, chest-shaking tears. A common fool ruining an otherwise splendid service.

I was livid. Hysteria is not noble.

And we had a closed casket again for Kristi Kenner. Now, little Kristi, she came from a well-off family, so one expected the best arrangements. Plenty of flowers, a proper car for the family. One imagines families like Kristi's, rich families, have an immunity to tragedy – a bubble over their whole lives. Nobody goes out, nobody comes in – nobody uninvited.

I understand they found her cut open – split down the left side from her breast all the way to her knees. She bled to death, under the viaduct. One is not supposed to know the details, but I heard that her entire body had been shaved clean with a hunting knife. Madmen, Your Eminence, madmen. I blame the government. The prisons today are about as secure as a chickadee nest on a telephone pole. So, we had a closed casket again.

What a mob scene at Kristi Kenner's service. Hundreds of girls from the high school, and each one brought her own candle, or a pink teddy bear, or the worst sort of handmade cards. All this trash piled a mile high on the church steps. The Kenner family did not spend three thousand dollars on quality floral arrangements to have them tarted up with gaudy pink carnations and green women's rights ribbons and plastic unicorns tied to yellow roses.

But those brats had no concern for the family or anyone else who appreciates a proper service. Oh no, the whole day was about them, all about those greedy little girls and their horrid flowers. The television cameras are never too far away from those girls.

Wait until it's one of their children, wait until they come home and find their baby girl skinned alive or their beautiful boy stuck like a pig on the sharp end of a fence-post – will they want two hundred screaming teenagers falling to the ground in front of the church and writhing like possessed Haitians?

The Reverend frets again with a third cigarette.

The MacAbee boy, out for a Saturday ride on his snowmobile. He must have felt free as the clouds. Such a handsome boy, too. So thin in the coffin. He looked like a Christian martyr. And the white lilies with white orchids on a white casket, simply overwhelming. His entire body glowed. He was a clean white star in the dark centre of the cathedral, as if all the light in the world was magnetized, drawn to him.

I had to touch him, you understand, Your Eminence, I had to. I needed to connect. I was shrinking, disappearing. I brought myself into his light. I'm hollow and there's a ringing inside me, so much of me is diminished. One touch, one step up to the casket, one clear look at the centre of the sun.

I tell you I was pulled, Your Eminence, pulled against my will!

I smelt violets. Clear as noon, the scent of purple violets. But there weren't any violets in his arrangement. The sugary, metallic scent of violets, it ate into my skin, it burned my eyes. The boy, Your Eminence, I tell you the boy was perfumed with violets – his body wasn't decaying, it was blossoming.

A miracle. The boy was incorruptible, Your Eminence, a true martyr. My first, after all these years. I needed more, more of his miracle. One more lungful. I lifted his head half an inch off the pillow … I was respectful … the violets –

They pulled me away, like a dog! Big ugly men with rough faces!

The violets were fading, ruined by their cheap soap and cheaper aftershave, ruined by dirty big hands. I cried out. I cried out to the boy's mother, she had to understand, she had to be proud – a miracle is a powerful consolation.

'Who are you?' she screamed. 'Who are you who are you who are you?'

I'm sorry, I told her I was sorry. 'Please forgive me,' I said. I tried to tell her – that boy is me, that boy is me. She kept screaming, screaming – 'Who are you why are you here who are you what are you doing here who are you?'

I tried to tell her, Your Eminence. I know about molecules and where bodies go, I know how the dead chastise unbelievers, I know about martyrs and saints and dead teenagers and schoolgirls and murder and accidents and the sign of the violets and dead teenagers and –

I'm not mad. I understand what other people see. I can see my own face, I can see my own wasted body. I tried to tell her about me.

She wouldn't stop screaming! Evil, jealous bitch!

Who am I, who am I, indeed!

She's like all the rest, she envies my calm. Accidents, disease, murderers, guns, whatever it is that kills – I face it, I face it down and find something gorgeous, something sweet and lasting and harmonious –

And yes, Your Eminence, something even you can't see, something most people can't. I see the promise of more. More light, more quiet, a garden of quiet. I have seen things in the simplest places that you and everyone else have overlooked. I have witnessed, Your Eminence, witnessed the transgressions of the body made as nothing, nothing. I have shared molecules with the dead.

Oh, you talk about the soul, you talk about the next life, you talk talk talk until you've deafened yourself! I have shared with the dead!

Take as much offence as you like, I'm tired of explaining the glories of Heaven to the minds of ants – yes, ants!

Go on, run off, run off and tell the church council that I'm mad, mad as a spring day, mad as a beehive. Do as you like! Coward! ... Do as you like.

Stands and lights a final cigarette, paces.

Do as you like. I have children to bury.

END

An Interview with RM Vaughan

by Kevin Connolly

Some quick questions about the genesis of the three monologues: which came first; did you write them separately and then see that they all went together; and did you rework them once you thought of them as a trilogy? Because there are things that pop up in all three if you look closely.

There are things that pop up. I think that's probably because I'm a hack and I rehash things over and over again *(laughs)*. The first one was *A Visitation by Saint Teresa of Avila upon Constable Margaret Chance*, which I wrote believing it was the beginning and the end of something. I wrote that piece specifically for Ann Holloway, who's one of my favourite actors, and it was directed by Franco Boni. It went off way better than we ever thought it would, so Franco said, 'Well, monologues seem to work for you. Why don't you write another one?' So then the next one was *The Susan Smith Tapes*, and that one went off even better.

But you were still thinking of them as separate pieces?

Not at that point. After the first one, because I had already written parts of *Susan Smith*, Franco said, 'I think this is a trilogy. I think you need to write three of these.' And from there I began to get the idea that these would be three women somehow engaged in the world of violence, but from very different viewpoints. And, in some ways, they represent the way we formalize violence in our society. We have justice, represented by the cop; we have a violent criminal in Susan Smith; and we have the spiritual and psychological idea of how we process violence, as represented by the reverend. The idea of knitting them together became more and more immediate to me. Even then, the last piece, *Dead Teenagers*, was originally written for a man – Peter Lynch.

Were all three written with a specific actor in mind?

Yes, they were.

When I was at the Ottawa Writers' Festival I was talking to this very interesting Icelandic playwright named Havar Sigurjonsson, who said that he can't write a play just thinking about the characters. The only way he can write a play is to imagine who might direct it and which actors would play which roles, and then to literally have them walk onto the stage in his head and start talking.

I have to do the same thing. I've always worked more or less with same cabal of actors – Kirsten Johnson, Peter Lynch, Moynan King as a director and before her Franco, Kirsten's sister Sigrid, Caroline Gillis, Michael Achtman and Veronika Hurnik a couple of times. It's the same thing, though; I have to see them in the parts. I don't know if I'm responding to something in the actors' personalities or whether part of me is just thinking, 'This would be so much fun to write for A, B and C,' but theatre makes me very anxious; or rather, the theatre world makes me very unhappy and anxious, and the only way I can deal with the theatre world is at some early stage to say, 'Here's all the people I would work with lined up in my head. All these nice, wonderful people I trust.'

Then you don't have to think of an asshole getting a hold of your script and putting the wrong people in the roles and wrecking everything.

Exactly. All that is wiped out and I can start.

And after the fact, does it matter so much who plays the parts?

It still does. It still pains me to see other people doing the parts *(laughs)*. I went to a production of *Camera, Woman* in Montreal, which was fine, but I didn't like most of the actors – I liked one, but not the others. Then I saw it done by another company in Ottawa and they were all good actors, but I just couldn't stop seeing Veronika and Ellen-Ray (Hennessy) in my head; I couldn't stop seeing these fantastic people. So, I don't know, it's hard.

I guess once you go through a production working with actors, they teach you a lot about your own script and it's hard to imagine anyone else doing it.

Absolutely, because you rewrite based even on simple things – their inflections, how they say a word, even. You try to build that in if you can. But in the case of *Dead Teenagers*, I originally wrote it for Peter and we did a workshop of the piece in a church – St. Stephen in the Field – and it came off well, people said they liked it. But the underlying thing people were getting was that the reverend was a pedophile. Which is not what the play's about. But there was just no way to get out from under that. I tried rewriting it again and again for a male character and there was absolutely no way to keep that from coming into people's heads.

You mean to make it clear that you were talking about a kind of ecstatic attention to the body rather than a sexualized attention?

I know that could be read as me saying women aren't sexual, but that's not what I mean. The problem is that the culture projects a kind of perverse pedophilia onto priests automatically now.

And there's not the same stigma. Even if you read the female priest's attention to the bodies as a sexual thing – which it's clear you shouldn't – it wouldn't ruin it in the same way as if the character were male.

I feel bad about it in a way, because Peter was so good in it. But I'll just have to write something else for Peter.

Is there a huge difference for you as a writer in how it comes out when you're writing a monologue as opposed to a multi-character play? For example, with a Pinter play, you can imagine the playwright writing it without identifying with any one particular character. But I would guess that's much more difficult with a monologue.

Actually, I find that I write them really quickly. I hate it when writers talk this way, but it is true – once I start hearing the voice in my head it just goes. I wrote *The Susan Smith Tapes* in one night. I worked with Moynan and sort of tinkered with it a little, but basically the bulk of it was written in one night. I did all my research, I read all the articles I could find on Smith, and I just tried to have this kind of possession moment where

I could think like her and away it went.

It must give you a kind of momentum, the economy of style that's required in a monologue.

Yes it does, because you're basically just talking onto the page.

That's something you don't get in a multiple-character drama?

No, because somebody has to respond. And there are too many rules. With multi-character plays I've been in enough workshops to know someone will always pick up a scene you think is dreamy and beautiful and poetic and they'll say, 'Well, there's no conflict here.' There are all these rules and dramaturgy and diagrams attached to those things, and I just don't want to do that any more. I have a couple of play ideas in my head – one's another monologue and there's another one for three people – and when I think about that one I think of very severely contained scenes. I don't see myself as a kind of Shavian writer where people are always batting things back and forth. I don't want to do big multi-character plays any more; they're just not for me.

So there's really a difference in kind between the two.

Another thing that comes into it that nobody likes to talk about is that if you want to get a multi-character play produced you need an enormous amount of money. And when there's an enormous amount of money acquired or that you need to acquire, then people feel they have more say in it. The more people onstage, the more you're inviting excessive outside input. There's something that's quite pure about one director, one writer, one actor. I've done enough things with

Moynan now that we're getting to the point that we don't even need to speak in full sentences. It's all shorthand now, and because we use actors we've worked with before, we know their strengths, we know how they like to work. I find it the same when I make films with Michael Achtman and Laura Cowell. We just made a film a few weeks ago and it was just like that. There's no dramaturgy, no excessive yakking – it just gets done.

With monologues – and I've seen them done well several times now – it starts with the writing but it's always a combination of acting, writing and directing. I think it was Tanja Jacobs, when I interviewed her at the Tarragon a couple of years ago, who pointed out something that should have been obvious to me, which was that every monologue is really a two-hander, with the audience as the scene partner. And the fact that the audience can't speak out has to be worked into both the performance and the writing.

You have to create spaces for the audience to digest the information, to create breathing room for them to absorb, in my case, the insane things people are saying. With the last one, *Dead Teenagers*, I'm not saying the acting was fast, but on opening night I felt that a lot of stuff was missed. But later as everything relaxed, that dialogue actually began between Caroline (Gillis) and the audience. I could feel the audience thinking with her, I could feel them absorbing. When *Susan Smith* was made into a film – I don't agree with this, but a couple of people have told me they found it too fast. Because of the constraints of the film, which was made for television, it had to be twenty-two minutes long. And it's a twenty-nine- or thirty-minute play. It doesn't seem like a lot of difference, but when you're absorbing information, it is. So I'd agree with

Tanja – in terms of a monologue, maybe the real question for a writer is making sure those spaces are built in. You actually have to break one of the primal rules of playwriting – which is that no words are wasted – and you actually have to give the audience words that they can ignore.

That's a rare admission. A lot of writers make out that everything is about distilling something. If you could write the same sentiment or evoke the same emotion with fewer words, that's always better. What I've always felt that position didn't acknowledge is writing as a temporal activity, in which you're always anticipating something is going to happen.

I hate that kind of playwriting. It's not writing, it's telegraphing. I hate it when I go to a play and it's just little beams of information shot at me.

It's very affected in some ways, and manipulative of the audience.

I think it only works in situations like, 'This is a play about the Westray mine disaster.'

These plays are not exactly polemical, but they are morality plays. And there seems to be an added tension for the audience here, especially in the first and third parts of the trilogy, because you've deliberately put them in a kind of exalted position. In Dead Teenagers *she's even addressing her discussion to someone she calls 'Your Eminence,' which could be God at the beginning but turns out to be someone higher up in the church; while in* The Susan Smith Tapes *she's addressing celebrity figures but also the audience.*

And she's addressing the camera.

A Visitation seems much more confrontational, and at the same time much more intimate. Was that something deliberate that came up during the writing of it, or was it something you recognized later? Because in The Susan Smith Tapes you make it an issue – she's very self-conscious about her presentation, she calls things 'set pieces' and talks about how 'natural' she appears on camera.

There seem to be several lines of thinking about this in the theatre. One of them is that you can't have the unknown being addressed, you have to have a specific creature. I don't actually believe that; I think when people sit down in the theatre they are already creatures. So, even if the actor is calling someone 'Your Eminence,' some people will quickly adopt a judgmental position, others will wonder who the hell is she talking to, still others will think, 'She's talking to a figure I can't really see' and agree to play along. Even when it's very pointed there are still limitless responses. So really, that technique – what's it called? the apostrophe? – we all know it; television commercials use it. It's a convention; I don't really have to do a lot of thinking about that. But in the case of Susan Smith, one of the things I discovered about her when I was researching the play was that she was obsessed with public attention and the media around her. It became very apparent while I was writing it that she was speaking to a direct media presence of some kind. Because the woman just did not live any other kind of life. Once she committed her crimes it seems like the rest of her life was mediated.

It's like she became completely dissociated from her self.

And still is, from what I continue to read about her.

Correct me if I'm wrong, but did you change her class a little?

No.

She was definitely from a lower-class background then. I get my child murderers mixed up.

She was from a lower-class background and a broken family.

Was postpartum depression involved?

Well, it depends what theory you believe in. There's the theory that she wanted to marry the town rich boy, who didn't want her kids, so she got rid of them. That's the mercenary theory. The one I'm most attracted to, and tried to work into the play, was a disorder called Boundary Confusion Disorder – it happens to a lot of young mothers, They feel hungry and they feed the kids, they feel sleepy, they put the kids to bed. That's the mild form of it. The mother can't tell the difference between her needs and the child's needs, and it is related to postpartum depression. It happens particularly with young mothers who have too many children too quickly. One of the more frightening thoughts about Susan Smith is that she wanted to kill herself and killed her kids instead. She actually said at one point that she was going to get into the car with them, and at the last second, didn't.

There's something about it that sort of rings true. In that case there seems to have been a certain amount of sympathy for her, generally, but you seem to have less than most. She's not a very likeable character as she appears here.

No, she's not. And she continues to be unlikeable. After I wrote the play I realized how many other 'products' there are out there about her. There's actually a musical floating around that played Off-Off-Broadway, and then Richard Price, the American novelist, wrote a novel about her, but his take was on the whole race element in the case. She originally told the police a black man had stolen her van and hijacked her kids and the police accepted it instantly and went on this ridiculous chase. Now, in hindsight, the police say they never really believed her. But I don't know if I'm sympathetic or not. I'll give you an anecdote about that. Kirsten hates me telling people about this, but too bad. Her mom and dad are great supporters of her – they come to everything. I really like them; her father's a philosophy professor and her mother's a psychiatrist of some kind. They're both really intelligent people, but they have a certain world view. So they come to the play and watch it with everyone else, and half the audience is thinking, 'Oh, this poor, messed-up creature, she's horrible but I can't help feeling sorry for her.' I was sitting in front of Kirsten's mother and father and afterwards he said, 'Well, that really had a lot to say about women and justice.' To which my first response, washed-up liberal that I am, was that he had had the liberal take on it, the 'poor nutcase killed her kids' take. Then he says, 'Yes, it's sad in this day and age a person wouldn't get the death penalty just because she's a woman' *(laughs)*. So he was taking this complete libertarian perspective – why should we feel any more sorry for her than we would for a male killer of children? Which was a completely valid response …

It just wasn't one you were expecting.

No. I first thought, 'Well, maybe I'm being really ambiguous here. Maybe I should figure out exactly what I want people to think.' But then I thought, 'No, because I really don't know what I think; how can I know what to think about someone who killed her own children?' There's a kind of demonic logic she has that I can trace, but I can never say I empathize with or comprehend.

There's a misunderstanding, about art in general and writing in particular, that you see a lot, which is the assumption that in order to write about something the writer must come to a conclusion about their subject. Whereas in fact it's often much more interesting if the writer just digs more deeply into the mess of ambiguity and ambivalence that these things bring up.

And, socially, there's nothing you can really do about a woman like Susan Smith. They could have put her to death – which I don't agree with, by the way – which would have accomplished nothing. It certainly wouldn't help anyone understand her actions any better. So she'll spend the rest of her life in prison, and we still won't know anything more about her, and it won't stop anyone from doing it again.

Towards the end of the monologue she's sort of arguing against capital punishment, saying her example could help all kinds of people over and over again. But in fact, it's serving as no example whatsoever. If anything, she's more perplexing with time.

And the fact she's become a creature of the media, in a weird way makes her a kind of criminal celebrity, so I don't know how exemplary that is, either.

I think the public is getting a little sick of that sort of celebrity. I don't know whether it peaked at O.J. or what.

Dar Heatherington is no Susan Smith.

But I like that story.

Yeah, I do too. She might be Part Four *(laughs)*.

You've gone out of your way to make all three 'monsters' women, and in two cases you've done it very pointedly in that the typical choice would have been to make them male. What were you trying to do there, particularly with the constable and the priest?

I was really inspired by Moynan King's play, *Bathory*. Not just because it's a great play, but because it came out at the peak of Homolka-Bernardo hysteria in Ontario. At the time the accepted thinking about Karla Homolka was she was an abused woman led into these evil deeds by her satanic husband. Some people still believe that; we're just not ready to accept the fact that a woman might enjoy being violent or participating in these horrors. When Moynan presented her play at Buddies I'll never forget this terrible review she got from that idiot Kate Taylor, who basically said – she didn't say it in this language but this was the gist – that the play was unconvincing because women don't behave in this way. And Moynan very publicly took the stand that yes, they do, that women are capable of violent acts. She was way ahead of her time in that, because now we know it, particularly with the Reena Virk thing and subsequent works by Joyce Carol Oates or, earlier, Margaret Atwood's *Cat's Eye*, which deals with how terrible little girls are to one another. We're beginning to understand that while it's a different capacity for violence, women have as much capacity for violence as men.

Also, I'm not very interested in writing about men. I've never really understood men, for lots of reasons, and I sometimes feel my male characters are often there just for comic purposes. They're not terribly sympathetic. In the play I wrote about Marcel Proust, Marcel is a great character but a lot of his talking is the high-art language of the aesthete that he was. It's very removed, while his mother comes off as this total powerhouse. So, in the end I just thought, 'Why am I fighting this? Why don't I just write about women – this seems to be what works.' There was a lot of talk about women and violence in the air at the time, and I thought a lot of it was very reductive. It seemed to come from the standpoint of, 'Well, women can't possibly be violent, but they are, so let's figure out why that is.' Which is a stupid circle.

Even some of the feminist literature approaches it by trying to put them into the position of being social victims. Women become violent because the society is patriarchal and inherently violent. It's a little like the extreme politically correct view of Native culture and history, where they were always supposed to be thinking of the environment, and, you know, never wasted a tooth from a beaver they ate and abhorred violence, when the truth was that many tribes were incredibly warlike, etc.

And what a terrible amount of pressure to be under. If you're a woman engaged in discussions about feminism – whatever wave of feminism it is: first wave, second wave, third wave – you're constantly having to negotiate between this essentialist nonsense that you're a woman and therefore part of nature, and somehow higher and removed, and this other position that says you can go fix the car, or dress like a man and be as butch as you want to be. And it's just back and forth, back and forth.

And there's a repression there of all kinds of aggression – which is a force that doesn't necessarily have to be negative. Aggression can be useful, but all you have to do is look at society to see that women are encouraged not to be aggressive.

Yes, and when they are aggressive their aggression is infantilized. It's cute, or it's something they did because they were hysterical and confused.

Or it's sex play.

Exactly. It's never premeditated, never something they thought about and then did. Women are not supposed to be calculating and evil. So I wanted to create characters who, at their core, are aware they were evil and calculating and are now figuring out why they do it. The reasons they do it might be insane, but they're not unaware of what they're doing.

They're all kind of confessions, aren't they? They all touch in troubling and bizarre ways on religious and moral and spiritual issues. Why's that exactly?

(Laughs) Well, it's good material. I've only lived in Ontario for about twelve years, and in the last seven or eight years I've noticed there's a real cult of morbid victim celebration. The specifics of this event won't mean anything by the time the book comes out, but there's been a recent murder of a child in Toronto and the newspapers have made a bundle of money off it. They've created the usual hysteria, which we all know about, but as we speak a mural is being made that's dedicated to this child's life. I guess at least people are making art out of it, which is fine. There will inevitably be some kind of book or film treatment. I don't have any problem with that, except that there's a tackiness to it that we never want to talk about. So I started thinking about all these funerals they have in

small communities, where a teenager dies tragically one way or another and everyone comes out with flowers and letters. I was fascinated by how pre-programmed that all was. When Princess Diana died, why did people know that the thing to do was to go to the Princess of Wales Theatre and leave flowers and candles and teddy bears? Where did we learn that, and how did that become instantly standardized? And in this recent case of the little girl being killed, everyone went to her school with candles and flowers and notes. The tropes just kicked in. It's an odd standardization of a grief practice.

It seems to be a kind of theatre, as well. I don't believe a lot of these people are feeling genuine grief for the person. In the same way as a lot of people who get angry driving around in their cars haven't been made angry about anything in particular – they just seem to feel the need to express anger.

Yes, they're performing anger. So my next thought was, if these things are kind of like art, or community theatre, then they have to have critics – all art has to have critics. So who could be a critic of these public expressions of grief and mourning? Well, perhaps it would be a reverend. And what would she have to say about them? You know, were the flowers tacky, were the cards well-written – how would someone break down these practices to their elements and decide whether it was tastefully done? And that's where *Dead Teenagers* came from – that fascination with this cycle of spectacle and performance.

All you have to do is look at American television to see their obsession with crime and punishment and an extreme form of morality. It leaks into our culture to a point where it seems almost the same, but what amazes me is how many things you look at that are inherently moral narratives and yet they don't discuss everyday ethics – you know, why do you fuck around on your spouse or lie to your boss or cheat on your taxes. No, they have to be about the most extreme cases: infanticide, sexual abuse, devil worship, whatever. Where do you think this obsession with broad, black-and-white morality comes from?

It comes from luxury. We don't have anything else to worry about. The Cold War is over, Apartheid has been dissolved, there is more or less a standard of equity in the West – more or less.

But the mentality is almost fifteenth-century.

In a way, yes, I agree with you. Whenever I watch those Jerry Springer television shows – you know, 'You cheated with my girl,' that sort of thing – I always think the audience is about one inch away from throwing rocks at the people on the stage. A culture can only afford that level of hair-splitting when it has literally nothing else to worry about. I really think we're in a very luxurious period in our history, though looking around it maybe doesn't feel like it sometimes. I'm sure if we were in India right now, we would not see people in the media having protracted discussions of infidelity or Supreme Court cases about kiddie pornography. They just don't have the time. I also think that 'issue plays' like that don't work anymore. I've been to a few issue plays lately and television seems to have taken away that energy. Theatre doesn't need that anymore.

We've touched on it earlier but didn't discuss it: all three plays also feature children or a child as a central issue. You do it quite cleverly because it lets you deal with two of society's biggest hot buttons, which are sexual morality and our foggy worries about the future, which we're all anxious about these days.

Well, for me, I'm queer and I'm never going to have children. So they're always speculative subjects for me – as speculative or alien as Mars might be, or writing about time travel. I feel like I have limitless licence on the topic because I'll never have one, which also means I'm freed from the need to get it right. And I feel that burdens a lot of writing about parents and children, because there is no way to get it right; every situation is different. Like most writers, I had a wacky childhood, and I guess I wasn't even aware it pops up so often, but people have pointed it out about my novels. They've told me, 'You know, Richard, you have a lot of traumatized children in your fiction.' I don't know why it's an issue, other than, again, it's just really good material.

I also wrote the last of these plays after *Camera, Woman* was out in the world and done. That was a play about ideas with a capital 'I,' a play where people basically stood around arguing about art and representation and questions of civil rights and legitimacy and how an act is represented. I still like that play a lot, but I needed to write something that was a lot messier, a lot more intimate, after this big Idea Play. I needed to get back to something that was more poetic, in a way. I guess one could be poetic about, I dunno, PCBs or something, but it's not in me.

But these ideas of motherhood and children and the future – you take children out of that and the arguments become much less complex.

And children are really easy to project onto – there's a built-in level of concern for the majority of the audience.

All three plays, even if they seem to have sensationalistic subjects, I think they're really more about ecstatic states, or even profane states. This has popped up elsewhere in your writing, and I wanted to ask you, first, about your own religious background, and how that's affected your work.

I have almost no religious background. My mother was raised Catholic and my father, as far as I know, had almost no religious upbringing. He was nominally Protestant. When my mother and father married she converted to the United Church – I mean, you don't even have to believe in God to be in the United Church. They were well into their middle age when my brother and I were brought into the home – we're both adopted, from different biological sources. So there were already levels of alienation from religion built in from the get-go. I think I went to the United Church Sunday school maybe four times. My father never went to church. My mother went because she likes to talk and all her old gals were there, and she was in the choir. I don't know how much devotion was behind this; all I can remember from church was colouring. I didn't have any profound religious experience. And I think precisely because of that I've always been drawn to liturgical art and to Catholicism particularly: the poeticism, the garish art, the lavishness, the sado-masochism and extremity of it. If you'd have come here two months ago I would have had all these devotional candles around the apartment (for some reason I got rid of them). I used to collect saints' candles, and I'm still very interested in Wiccan practices, though I would not identify as a Wiccan.

Do you sometimes wonder where that comes from?

I know exactly where it comes from. I'm afraid of losing my mind – all the time. And if there's a system out there that will allow me to make some sense ... or not even sense, but will allow me to have a set of gestures that will ward off evil-slash-insanity, then I'm going to go find that system.

So it's the theatricality of the religion that attracts you?

No, it's actually the participation. What draws me to Catholicism is certainly not the evil Catholic Church itself, or its administrators, it's the idea that you can go in front of a picture of a saint and you can light a candle and there's communication. I actually find it quite easy to believe in saints; I can believe there were people who were so psychically powerful or so psychically fucked up that they could reach a higher plane. I'm also attracted to Wiccan practice because you can mix stuff in a pot and go and burn it out in the woods, and then someone who's been bugging you will go away. I like that kind of cause-and-effect relationship to religion – it's ritualized narrative, and it's active. I have no attraction to Buddhism or yoga, all these Eastern things everyone in the West gets into. People are attracted to them because there's no activity, it's all on a higher plain. If I were going to have a religious experience I would not want it to be pure and clean and stark; I'd want it to be baroque, and messy, and cluttered and ridiculous.

I reacted very badly to religion eventually, even though it was never really pushed on me. I'm an avid atheist at this point, but I wonder sometimes in my rejection of it whether it has a greater hold or effect on me than it might have had if I'd just gone to church in the usual disengaged way most people do.

If you have an uncomplicated relationship to your faith then it's not much more intriguing to you than your diet or your work. But I'm a bit of a cultural shopper. And the things I like about a religion are the holidays and the food, the things that are tangible.

Like all of the plays I've read of yours, these three have minimal stage directions. Are you just very conscious of the collaborative side of theatre or is there sort of a minimalism at work?

There's no minimalism at work; I think that in most cases minimalism actually means you're just cheap and lazy. I've also had many experiences with directors in which they pay absolutely no attention to the stage directions, so I'm just wasting my breath. If you're looking at a play as a written text, then you have to look at what stage directions are adding. I edit an imprint of plays for Broken Jaw Press – all new Canadian plays. And sometimes people give me their scripts and the stage directions are telegraphed. You know, 'Dark. Night. Sound outside.' And I have to tell them, 'This needs to be a sentence. This is going to be a book now, it's going to be read.' And they don't get that. They've never looked at a script as anything other than a step to a production.

I've always liked reading plays, even before I saw a lot of theatre. It's a different experience. Reading Shakespeare is just as satisfying as seeing Shakespeare.

It's often more so. For people to pretend that when they're reading a play they're not engaged in the same way as they are reading any other type of fiction is silly. On the other hand, I've had the experience of having plays directed where people have just done whatever the hell they wanted with the stage directions. So in that sense, if you can't control them, what's the point?

Can you speak a little about the miracle play that frames the second piece? Who is St. Teresa, and why did she have to be there, in your mind?

St. Teresa of Avila was a scholar and a great intellect, and what she brought to the Catholic Church, and Christianity in general, was the practice of thinking through your religion. That's why she was such a revolutionary, and why she's often represented with symbols that mean wisdom. She serves as a counterpoint to Margaret Chance, the main character, whose belief system has been on automatic pilot her whole life. She's never investigated why she believes certain things about certain ethnic groups. She's never investigated why she believes certain things about the church, or about violent behavior, or spandex pants – all these crazy things she believes. But then something weird happens in her life. Her child is beginning to act strangely and she's suddenly frightened. She needs to investigate what's happening but she hasn't got the tools. So, here's this creature who exists outside her, and who she can see only at the end of the play, who is a symbol of investigation. I guess the audience needs to have a certain level of hagiography to fully get it, but on the other hand, when it was staged and the miracle visions occurred, it actually gave people a chance to breathe, to take a break from Chance's barrage. It's something outside of Margaret, something that tells the audience the writer is not in sympathy with

Margaret. It's also on some level a distancing device. We need distance from her – she's too confrontational, she's too overpowering. When it was staged it was interesting to see how much people liked her, and found her hilarious, until she starts getting really unpleasant and actually nuts at the end, and then the audience, on a dime, turned on her. That was hard for the actor to do. Because she could feel that every night, she could feel them giving her all their love and then suddenly hating her at the end. Ann was exhausted at the end of that play, and so was Kirsten with *Susan Smith*. It was really exhausting for both of them.

All three are a workout for both actor and audience, I think. Because you're clearly pushing the audience towards a position where they're either making judgments or conscious of being in a position where most people would make judgments, or where judgment itself is an issue. Their discomfort has to be part of it. But I guess it's just as uncomfortable for an actor to be judged for thirty minutes.

But it's also just an extension of what every play does. The second someone walks onstage you go, 'Look at her shoes, look at her hair, look at her body size – what are they saying?' I guess I just tried to extend that judgment period and focus it as much as possible.

In A Visitation*, there's a real rough humour to the play, and I was wondering to what extent the comedy takes the edge off, and to what extent it just creates more tension.*

Oh, I don't think it takes any edge off. It's sneaky …

Because you can deal with more awkward material like

homophobia and racism more easily with a joke than you can playing it straight, even if that joke is offensive.

Granted. The alternative would have been to simply lecture the audience by showing us a racist cop with no sense of humour.

Which would have been tedious and we've seen that already.

Right, we know there are bad cops and we've seen them before. So the humour of the play is sneaky in that it makes Margaret likeable. Even at her worst, she's likeable. So you have to process it: 'I like this person, even though I hate everything that she's saying.'

Well, there are people who are like that – people who have at least one thing about them that makes you want to never speak to them again. But that doesn't mean you can't learn anything from people like that, can't ever enjoy their company, or that you don't have to put up with them at family functions. You can't just be forever correcting people on their behaviour or you'll turn into one of those people yourself.

I think it was also important, again, that this was coming from a woman. We have to learn that these things are generated by all levels of the population, not just a nasty group of white men who work in the government or the police department. It doesn't come out of nowhere. To pretend otherwise is actually more dangerous than trying to let it out. I've had to explain that play, *A Visitation*, to people who were wondering if I was advocating a certain kind of racism. Sometimes audience members are not that smart. It's tedious, but sometimes you do have to explain yourself as an artist. I had to tell people that if they make it to the end of the play they'll realize she has this big worry that her family has something genetically wrong with them, that there's a psychotic element in her gene pool. And then you realize that all these anxieties she has about ethnic mixing and purity come from this core fear.

I asked you yesterday on the phone if these plays have ever been played together …

And they haven't.

And you wondered what theatre company would be willing to take them on. To me, it reads like a whole unit – when I was reading it, I wasn't even thinking of it as a trilogy; it read more like a triptych. I wondered if you could talk about that and about the frustration playwrights sometimes have about getting risky material like this produced.

I'm not really frustrated yet, because all of them were produced at least once, and one of them (*The Susan Smith Tapes*) was made into a short film by Jeremy Podeswa, and it's on TV constantly, about every two months. So I'm not really frustrated about it. I would like to see them produced as one evening, however a director would configure that – there are various ideas floating around. At this point I think there would be two problems. I would have to present it to an artistic director who had already had some sort of relationship to my work, because approaching those scripts cold would be a bit difficult, particularly *A Visitation*. I think if it was read without any context for the work it would just be, 'No way, we're not touching this.' My dream would be to get some small pile of money together, do it in a rented situation and self-produce it. What I have no desire to have happen, and it's happened to me before, is have a big theatre company come along and give me a big cheque and say, 'Now we'll do your show!' and then wreck it. I'm never going through that again, and maybe that's why I'm writing monologues now. Because when there's one actor and one director I have a better chance to have some control over how it's going to be presented onstage.

Acknowledgements

None of these plays would have reached the stage without the loving support of my good and talented friends. Many thanks to Franco Boni, Ann Holloway, Moynan King, Kirsten Johnson, Caroline Gillis, Sky Gilbert, Peter Lynch, Sarah Stanley and David Oiye.

Sonja Mills wrote *The Danish Play*, which is currently enjoying a fabulous international tour. Her previous works are far less respectable.

Kevin Connolly is a writer, editor and former lead theatre writer for Toronto's *eye Weekly*. His most recent book is the poetry collection *Happyland* (ECW, 2002).

About the Author

RM Vaughan is a Toronto-based writer and video artist originally from New Brunswick. He holds a master's degree in English from the University of New Brunswick, and has lived in Saint John, Fredericton, Ottawa and Montreal. Vaughan's books include the poetry collections *A Selection of Dazzling Scarves* and *Invisible To Predators* (both ECW Press), the novels *A Quilted Heart* (Insomniac Press) and *Spells* (ECW Press) and the play *Camera, Woman* (Coach House Books). Vaughan was the 1994–95 Playwright-in-Residence at Toronto's Buddies in Bad Times Theatre, where most of his plays have been staged. Vaughan's essays, poems, short stories and plays appear in over thirty anthologies, and he writes about art and culture for a diverse group of periodicals, including the *Globe and Mail, The National Post, Saturday Night, Canadian Art, This, Lola, Toronto Life* and *Xtra*. Vaughan maintains a parallel career as a video artist. His videos and short films have played in festivals and galleries across Canada and around the world.

Typeset in Granjon and printed and bound at the Coach House on bpNichol Lane, 2003.

Edited by Alana Wilcox
Cover design by Ian McInnis
Cover image is from the film *The Susan Smith Tapes*, still by Carol Racicot, courtesy of da da kamera / Rebel Films
Photo pages 51 and 53 by Tod Bricker
Photo pages 17, 18, 20, 22 and 25 from the film *The Susan Smith Tapes,* stills by Carol Racicot, courtesy of da da kamera / Rebel Films

Coach House Books
401 Huron Street (rear) on bpNichol Lane
Toronto, Ontario
M5S 2G5

1 800 367 6360

mail@chbooks.com
www.chbooks.com